Social Skills Every Shy Kid Should Know

Unlock Your Social Superpowers and Slay the Shyness Monster

Hayden Fox

© Copyright - All rights reserved.

The content contained within this book may not be reproduced, duplicated or transmitted without direct written permission from the author or the publisher.

Under no circumstances will any blame or legal responsibility be held against the publisher, or author, for any damages, reparation, or monetary loss due to the information contained within this book, either directly or indirectly.

Legal Notice:

This book is copyright protected. It is only for personal use. You cannot amend, distribute, sell, use, quote or paraphrase any part, or the content within this book, without the consent of the author or publisher.

Disclaimer Notice:

Please note the information contained within this document is for educational and entertainment purposes only. All effort has been executed to present accurate, up to date, reliable, complete information. No warranties of any kind are declared or implied. Readers acknowledge that the author is not engaged in the rendering of legal, financial, medical or professional advice. The content within this book has been derived from various sources. Please consult a licensed professional before attempting any techniques outlined in this book.

By reading this document, the reader agrees that under no circumstances is the author responsible for any losses, direct or indirect, that are incurred as a result of the use of the information contained within this document, including, but not limited to, errors, omissions, or inaccuracies.

Claim your free gifts!

(My way of saying thank you for your support)

Simply visit **haydenfoxmedia.com** to receive the following:

- 10 Powerful Dinner Conversations To Create Amazing Kids

- 10 Magical Affirmations To Help Kids Become Unstoppable in Life

(you can also scan this QR code)

Table of Contents

Introduction 6

Chapter 1: What Feeds the Monster Inside You? 11

Chapter 2: It's Not Me, It's You...Feeding the Monsters 44

Chapter 3: Conquer Your Emotions 50

Chapter 4: Mindset 94

Chapter 5: You Are Wasting Your Time Being Shy 113

Chapter 6: Get Better Everyday .. 122

Conclusion 136

Introduction

Shyness can be a *monster*.

It can be a horrendous beast that can sit on your shoulders or on your chest when your teacher asks you to answer a question in class. Shyness can be a behemoth when you have to introduce yourself to a new group of friends during school break or when you go to a new school. Shyness can be an incubus when your parents want to drag you off to see some new family friends you've never met, while all you want to do is watch your favorite TV show.

It feels like the ground is being pulled out from under your feet when you hear someone say that it is normal to feel a bit nervous about a presentation, a test, or new people. It can become antagonizing knowing that your friends don't feel like you do at all. You feel angry when your gran or grandad says their new, uninvited guests don't bite. However, the *shyness-monster* is chewing on your head right there as you try to utter a simple "hello."

And even worse, shyness can really make you feel...well, lots of things. These feelings feel unnecessary, but they have such a hold on you that they paralyze you physically in confrontation—or even worse, leave you defenseless even if you have a great comeback.

Being shy is not a train crash or the end of the world though, despite it feeling like that. You also do not have to stick a fake smile on your face and push through meeting new people like Mom and Dad says you must. Envision shyness as the Joker to your Batman, the Lord Voldemort to your Harry Potter, The Green Goblin to your Spiderman...you get the gist. With a training montage and a cool theme song, you will be able to kick its butt in a matter of days!

Let me tell you a secret: your shyness is probably not even your fault.

Lots of things can make you shy—and I am not talking about presentations, meeting new people, and all those stressful situations. I'm talking about your personality type, your genetics, and your home.

You might be shy because you are an introvert, and there is nothing wrong with that! Everyone has different hobbies and interests and reacts differently in different situations. Some people prefer to spend time with their friends, talking and being social. Other people prefer to read books, play video games, or watch Netflix and hang out by themselves. There is no such thing as a right or wrong type of person; you're just a person with different interests.

You can't just learn how to stop being shy, much like you also can't just jump into the deep end of the pool if you don't know how to swim. You just have to remember that it is okay not to be able to swim at first because you can learn how to swim along the way.

Today you're a fish outta water, but tomorrow or the next day you could be swimming like Aquaman or The Little Mermaid; they don't think swimming is difficult, right? Once upon a time, swimming was probably a bit of a challenge for you, because you were small, and the deep end of the pool was where the dads used to hang out to hide from the moms at a family barbecue. Today, it's the perfect place to cannonball.

Shyness is the same. It is difficult to overcome today, probably a bit frightening, and you might need some lessons to combat it, but with some patience, time, and guidance, you might just be able to cannonball into a crowd one day to start a conversation—or even become that rockstar everyone said you couldn't be.

It is okay to be scared when you have to meet new people. It is okay when you stutter during your presentation because your heart felt like it was beating 500 beats per second. It is also important to remember that you won't wake up and magically have to be a rockstar or actor, because even they need to first master their crafts.

But how do you slay this shyness monster?

Do you have to gain XP in life by completing a side quest for a friendly goblin? Is there a special course after school no one tells you about? Is there a solution in the vitamins your mom gives you, but you forget to drink them every night? Or will it be one of those things where you wake up one morning, and it will be gone?

In this book, I am going to teach you exactly *why* you are shy and how to slay this horrendous, level-500 *shyness monster*.

Chapter 1: What Feeds the Monster Inside You?

Never feed the gremlins after midnight, we all know that. So why give the *shyness monster* any food when you know it is just going to bite you later?

It is important to learn why you feel scared or uncomfortable in a situation. *What is feeding this gremlin?* How can I stop feeding it...or at least how can I put this gremlin on a diet? Sometimes, you aren't even feeding this emotional gremlin that is hiding in your heart; lots of other things could be feeding it.

Being born shy is not uncommon; it's like sand on a beach—always present and sometimes quite irritating. Some babies are born with a gremlin of shyness in their hearts, often clinging and hiding behind their parents to find comfort, which moms and dads are very good at providing. Some of these babies outgrow their gremlins, leaving them behind along their journey as they grow and learn to walk, but other babies, unfortunately, hold onto their gremlins like it is the last cookie in the jar (and these gremlins love eating cookies to become little monsters). Other times, babies aren't even born shy, but due to their circumstances, they become consumed by their own artificial gremlins of shyness.

It is important to note that your shyness is *not your fault*. Shyness is not something that you can control or run away from. You can, however, face your shyness monster, and, with the right tools, you can easily take it down.

Let's dive into some reasons why you could be shy.

What's Your Personality Type?

Every person on earth has personality traits. According to Jamie Birt (2022), personality traits are characteristics and qualities that define you as a unique individual. This makes you different than Joe sitting next to you in science class.

Unlike in your favorite video game, you do not get to choose these characteristics, but rather develop them through your experience points as you grow up.

You get 5 big personality traits. These traits are known as OCEAN:

- Openness,
- Conscientiousness,
- Extroversion,
- Agreeableness, and
- Neuroticism.

All of these traits, in some way or another, affect the way you perceive the world, and your perception of the world, people, and places leads to anxiety, fear, and embarrassment, which leads to shy behavior.

A good place to start is to identify where you lie on the scale of these five traits and how to minimize your weaknesses and maximize your strengths.

Openness

What Is Openness?

How willing are you to try that new doughnut at Krispy Kreme? If you'd rather opt for your usual chocolate icing and frappuccino option, then you value comfort over new, exciting options, and that's okay!

See, openness is like a door in your mind, except this door does not close when a new person or new item is delivered to the door. The door is always open to accept and look at these new and exciting things. Openness is your willingness to try new things, even if it is only wearing a new shirt to school or eating a vegetable that you have despised since kindergarten. It is your eagerness to learn and try new things and explore–like your inner Indiana Jones or Dr. Smolder Bravestone.

If you prefer your weekends to look the same every week instead of going on random adventures with your friends, there's nothing wrong with you. You just prefer a steady, consistent routine because it is familiar. Familiarity is very comfortable.

Openness is not only just about opening the Jumanji board to go on a new adventure; it is also about creativity, curiosity, perspective, and change. Openness is an exceptionally great quality to have in life because it can assist you in the future with creative problem-solving, or even with having a better understanding of people because you are curious about their opinions.

If you are an open person, then you are more inclined to like art and express yourself in one way or another, either through painting, music, or writing. Some introverts find themselves buried in the arts quite deeply, often keeping it to themselves, but expression through art can be a wonderful way to introduce some openness into your life.

Shyness and Openness: Not Mortal Enemies, but Co-existors

Shyness is the way you feel backstage: nervous and scared that something bad might happen and that the audience might boo you off. On the other hand, openness is the excitement of going on stage to showcase your unique talent. Openness is the way you imagine you'll feel on stage: with an audience so impressed that they applaud and embrace your unique talent.

Becoming open is not going to happen overnight, but it is a quality that you can train into your life. Your shyness might be a little gremlin that terrorizes you, but it can also be a cute little golden retriever puppy that you can train. To perform at a talent show, you have to practice. The way you train a puppy is exactly the way you should compare yourself to exposing yourself to more open mindedness–your shyness is the puppy and you are the trainer. You can train your shyer self to be more open towards new experiences.

One Step at a Time

Start small by joining a club. A club is a place where you can share your interests with people who like similar things, and chances are that they are shy, too. Sometimes, it could be a bit easier to open up to new people with similar interests, because you have something in common to talk about.

Joining an online club or support group is also an option, especially if you are scared about going to a new place that you are not familiar with. In this way, you can socialize with people in a new space, but from the comfort of your home.

To open up a bit more, try a new activity. If you have always wanted to start a dance class, painting class, or new sport, now is the time to start. Starting a class would ease you into social situations because the sole focus of the class is not actually socializing, but the activity that everyone is there for. In that way, you might help your fellow artist, dancer, or athlete, and this can spawn a pretty organic friendship that is not forced. There is usually a teacher involved as well, assuring a monitored, controlled environment. If you are uncomfortable with any situation, you have a teacher to go to to express your discomfort, and they will definitely want to help you feel more comfortable.

Other than that, try small activities outside your comfort zone. This does not mean auditioning for the leading role of the school play or participating in pageants, but maybe auditioning to be a background character or volunteering to be a part of the decor team. By being a part of the team, you have to mingle with others to work on something together. Working with others is rewarding and will make you feel successful because you might not be acting center stage, but at least you painted the tree in the background and built the chair that the leading role is sitting on in front of a whole crowd.

Each small risk you take makes it more comfortable for you to step out of your comfort zone.

Conscientiousness

Conscientiousness is a *superpower*. It is a person's ability to be diligent, responsible, and organized. Conscientiousness is the ability to be considerate when it comes to other people's thoughts, emotions, and feelings. Conscientious people are always aware of their surroundings, how their behavior makes others feel, and how to help others.

You can see your parents or guardians being conscientious all the time. Your parents always check in on you, and they are always aware of you, even if you try to escape from them in your room. They make sure that you get enough sleep even if you don't feel like you need to go to bed early. They make sure that you are clean and that you have food in your belly, even if you're not hungry, and they always check in to make sure you do fine in school. Even if you try to escape what you perceive as control, they make sure you get to the mall and back safely because they are always aware of you, and they always care for you.

An example of *not* being conscientious is waiting until 9 PM to ask your mom for glue when you need it for a project that is due for the next day, or forgetting to message your parents that you made it home safely after going on a Target trip with your best friend.

Conscientiousness is an amazing skill to have when you have to face the horror show that is high school. If shyness is gremlins, high school *must* be Godzilla. High school is going to be a lot more demanding when it comes to your social battery, workload, and responsibilities. How are you supposed to juggle all of that when you can barely ask your teacher to help you with math?

How Conscientiousness Can Be Your Superpower

Conscientiousness can be found in pretty much anyone, but it develops in a pretty weird way. As a kid, you are more conscientious towards the people around you—you want to share your meal with your mom, hug your dad, and make sure that everyone is okay. You are always aware of people around you, even your siblings. You do things with purpose and love. As you age into your teen years, you become less conscientious with all the uncomfortable changes like puberty and going to high school. It is difficult to be considerate towards others when so much is going on, and you're trying to find yourself. When you reach young adulthood, your conscientiousness climbs again and never stops until the day you're old and frail in a retirement home.

Conscientiousness and shyness might have contrasts, but when you train yourself, you can become a master Jedi and use it to your advantage.

A great analogy for shyness and conscientiousness is Obi-Wan and Anakin from Star Wars. Obi-Wan is assertive, in control, and organized. He is a very skilled Jedi who often leads in combat with his ability to observe, then acts upon his observations when he plans how he'll engage in a battle or rescue others. Anakin though, at the beginning of his story, is impulsive and brash. He lets his emotions control him and lets them determine how he engages in his battles; this sometimes works, but most of the time it leads him down a path that is undesirable, such as getting captured. Obi-Wan tries to teach Anakin that, with a little bit of self-love, patience, and training, he can become an exceptional warrior if he can control his emotions. (Unfortunately, this obviously doesn't end up working out so well for Anakin!)

Learning the ability to control your shyness, as well as being able to observe each situation and act with patience instead of running away, is the first step to not becoming Darth Vader.

Train Yourself to Let Go of Everything You Fear to Lose —Master Yoda

You can use conscientiousness to your advantage to control the Force. Conscientiousness and shyness differ in the fact that shyness often leaves you avoiding social situations and any opportunity that contains some social interaction, especially when it comes to schoolwork and groups. Conscientiousness, on the other hand, wants to get your project or commitment over the finish line. It wants you to complete your project, regardless of if it means you must talk to a group or a class.

In this way, conscientiousness can push you outside of your comfort zone, outside the box you hide in. Conscientiousness and focus also differ. Conscientiousness is about your overall work ethic and responsibility, while focus is about being able to concentrate on a task without getting sidetracked.

Shyness might keep you back from excelling and being the best version of yourself because you focus on the fact that you are shy. Your shyness makes you self-conscious and scared, afraid that your group members and friends might judge you or think less of you, so you hyperfocus on it. Conscientiousness, on the other hand, will force you to complete the task that you were given and put aside the emotional drama going on in your head.

You can kick shyness' butt purely by focusing on completing your tasks, because when you focus on your work and focus less on your desire for social acceptance, you might just pick the fruit of reward from the apple tree you planted.

Conscientiousness is that adult voice in your head that says you need to get things done, no matter what. Because conscientiousness forces you to prioritize or plan, you identify what the most important thing is. For example, if you decide now that shyness is something you need to combat and that it is very important because you would like to audition for a school play to be something other than a background tree, your conscientiousness will force you to look at how to combat shyness. You will find yourself prioritizing getting out of your comfort zone as much as possible to get over the hill that is shyness.

Extraversion

Are you Squidward Tentacles, or are you SpongeBob SquarePants?

Extraversion is the ability of a person to be energized and charged in the company of other people. Extroverts are individuals who enjoy socializing and being around people, and who bloom in conversation.

Extroverts are exceptionally easy to identify in society. Not only because they have a crowd of people wrapped around their pinkies as they flatter and control the conversation, but also because their energy is just *electric*. Introverts and extroverts are like day and night.

Introverts, on the other hand, are people who get energized when they spend time alone or with a smaller group of people. Introverts prefer observing larger groups during social situations, and they prefer not to take part in the conversation, but to think about it. Introverts prefer to spend quality time with close friends and family, whereas extroverts would rather socialize as much as possible, regardless of whether they are close to them or not.

Shyness and introvertedness walk hand-in-hand most of the time. Shyness is a side-effect of introversion.

Your shyness does not determine your ability to be extroverted. Extraversion is not black and white. How many times do you find yourself extremely energized in a conversation with your good friends, sister, or parents, but completely quiet when it comes to a large group or new people? What is stopping you from being exactly like you are with your parents and friends in new groups or in front of a crowd of new people?

The answer is simple: your shyness.

Opposites Attract

Sometimes, you don't need a guide on how to get out of your box when you are shy, but you need *someone* to help you. A friend can be a great person to adapt and help you to slowly become a bit more outgoing. They can guide you out of your comfort zone and hold your hand in doing so.

Introverts and extroverts attract one another and build strong friendships, but it is not ideal when you want to stay in your comfort zone. As an introverted friend, you might find yourself stepping back when conversation arises to allow your extroverted friends to speak on your behalf. You might allow your parents to order your food at a restaurant or tell your mom what is wrong with you when you have to go to the doctor, so she can relay the message. Sometimes being shy can feel like playing The Whisper Game.

Introverts and extroverts bring out the best qualities in each other, and this could help you open at least just the lid of the box that you are hiding in as a shy person.

Introverts and extroverts can even out each other's wildly different energy. An extrovert can bring some excitement and enthusiasm into your life when it comes to social interactions, while you can be the support and calm energy that your friend needs.

Extroverts enjoy talking but sometimes find themselves ignored or overlooked in conversations. This could break down their self-esteem. Consider yourself the emotional support friend. As an introvert, you like listening, and you provide your extroverted friend with the comfort of someone who listens and cares. Conversations can be very meaningful and reflective, and you will find yourself in a good situation with a good friend.

When you have an extroverted friend, this friend could help you step out of your comfort zone by convincing you to go to bigger gatherings and parties. Your friend could even encourage you to try new things. That will force yourself to step out of your comfort zone to be more open.

Agreeableness

Agreeableness is the character that describes how friendly, kind, and cooperative you are towards other people. We all have different characteristics, otherwise known as personality traits, that distinguish us from others—it's the reason you act different from your sibling or neighbor.

Agreeableness is about being nice and getting along well with people. When someone is agreeable, they tend to be caring and considerate. They enjoy being around others and making new friends. They try to understand how others feel and are always ready to help when someone needs it. Agreeableness is the act of helping your friend with homework, saying please and thank you, and listening and paying attention.

Sometimes, people can be both disagreeable and friendly, even though it might sound a little confusing. It's like Shrek the Ogre; sometimes he is nice, but on other days, he is really mean and difficult. When someone is disagreeable, it means they don't always agree with what others say or do. They have their own opinions and aren't afraid to express them. But being disagreeable doesn't mean that they're mean or unfriendly.

On the other hand, being agreeable means being nice, kind, and sociable with others. It means enjoying spending time with people, being welcoming, and showing care for others' feelings.

How can someone be both disagreeable and friendly? Well, it's about finding a balance. Even if they disagree with someone, they can still be friendly by treating others with respect and kindness. They can have nice conversations, listen to what others have to say, and try to understand their perspective, even if they don't agree with it. It's about being nice and staying true to themselves at the same time.

People have different personalities, and sometimes they can have traits that seem a bit contradictory. But that's what makes us unique!

By being friendly and respecting others' opinions, even when we disagree, we can build better relationships and learn from each other, supporting someone who needs it.

People who are very agreeable are good at working together with others and being part of a team. They listen to different ideas, respect other people's opinions, and try to find solutions that everyone can agree on. They value collaboration and cooperation, and they're willing to contribute their ideas and efforts to achieve common goals. Being a team player is important to them, and they enjoy the satisfaction of working well with others.

Agreeable individuals prefer peace and harmony. They try to avoid arguments and conflicts by being understanding and finding peaceful ways to solve problems. They believe in treating others with kindness and respect, even when they have different opinions. They value fairness and seek to find solutions that are beneficial for everyone involved.

Politeness and consideration are key characteristics of agreeable people. They use kind words, say "please" and "thank you," and show good manners. They care about how others feel and try not to say or do things that might hurt them. They strive to create a positive and pleasant atmosphere when interacting with others. However, sometimes they are too nice which leads to them being taken advantage of or not standing up for themselves. Therefore, one must always have balance between being kind and polite, and not being taken advantage of or letting others walk all over you.

It's important to remember that everyone has their own unique combination of personality traits, and being agreeable is just one aspect of a person's character. Some people may naturally be more agreeable than others, and that's okay. We should appreciate and respect each other's personalities and find ways to work together, be kind, and treat one another with understanding and consideration.

Shyness vs. Agreeableness

Sometimes, shy people may have a lot of agreeableness inside them, but their shyness makes it harder for them to show it. They might want to be kind and helpful, but they may feel too shy to speak up or to approach others. Shyness can make it difficult for them to express their agreeable qualities openly.

However, once shy individuals feel more comfortable and confident, they can show their agreeableness more easily. As they become more familiar with people and their surroundings, their natural kindness and willingness to help others can shine through.

It's important to understand that being shy doesn't mean that someone is not agreeable. Shyness is just a temporary feeling that can make it harder to show agreeableness right away. Everyone is different, and some people may take more time to open up and show their agreeable qualities.

Remember, both agreeableness and shyness are just parts of a person's unique personality. It's important to appreciate and respect each other's differences and create a supportive environment where everyone feels comfortable being themselves.

Use Agreeableness to Your Advantage

One way that agreeableness can help is by building connections with others. When you approach interactions with kindness and a genuine interest in others, it creates positive connections, which can reduce the anxiety and self-consciousness that often come with shyness.

Another great thing about being agreeable is that it involves being a good listener. This means that you focus on what the other person is saying and really pay attention. By being a good listener, you shift the focus away from yourself and your shyness, and instead, you engage in genuine conversations that can help you feel more at ease.

Did you know that agreeable kids are often great at working in teams? Collaboration and teamwork are part of being agreeable. By participating in group activities or projects, you get to work with others in a cooperative and supportive environment. This allows you to communicate your ideas, listen to others, and contribute to a shared goal. Over time, this teamwork can help you feel more comfortable and gradually overcome your shyness.

Being agreeable means having empathy and understanding for others. This means that you can relate to how others feel and understand their experiences. Developing empathy helps you navigate social situations with more confidence and sensitivity. When you show kindness and understanding towards others, it creates deeper connections and reduces your shyness.

Overcoming shyness takes time and practice, especially if you are agreeable. Agreeableness sometimes is our downfall as shy kids, because we tend to always say "yes," to always agree, and to be nice even when someone is rude to us. As shy kids, we try not to argue and avoid conflict because we find it extremely difficult to speak up and defend ourselves.

Sometimes, we should not try to be more agreeable, but instead protect ourselves by being less agreeable. As we have mentioned before, you can be disagreeable and friendly. By using your disagreeableness, you can protect yourself from a situation where you need to stand up for yourself.

Neuroticism

Imagine that you have a superpower that allows you to feel emotions very strongly. Sometimes, you might feel happiness and excitement like a burst of confetti and balloons! However, neuroticism isn't exactly the type of superpower that turns you into Superman, The Flash or Wonder Woman. It is the type of superpower that can turn you into an evil Dr. Doofenshmirtz. Neuroticism doesn't focus on all your emotions, just on your bad emotions.

Neuroticism is all about how strongly we feel negative emotions and how we express them. Some people have a high level of neuroticism, which means that they experience emotions like a rollercoaster ride with lots of ups and downs and focus most of their energy on negative feelings like anxiety, sadness, anger and insecurity. People who have a higher level of neuroticism might act more extreme when it comes to situations that heighten their negative emotions.

For example, imagine that your friend accidentally spills some juice on their favorite shirt. If they have high neuroticism, they might feel really upset and get very worried about what others will think. They might dwell on it for a long time, even though it was just a little accident. It's like their emotional radar is super sensitive and picks up on even the tiniest blips!

On the other hand, some people have low neuroticism, which means that they tend to have a more stable and calm emotional experience. They might not get as easily bothered by small things and can quickly bounce back from setbacks. Consider it a superpower to overcome and lower your neuroticism, because taking control of your emotions requires you to be a superhuman.

Now let's imagine that one of your other friends spilled the exact same juice on their favorite shirt. They might be disappointed about the shirt, but they won't let it ruin their day. They'll brush it off, maybe even make a joke about it, and move on with a smile. Their emotional radar doesn't go haywire for every little thing, and they don't allow this one small negative experience to ruin the rest of their day.

It's important to remember that having high or low neuroticism doesn't make someone good or bad. It's just a part of who we are, like different colors on our emotional palette. Some people might be more sensitive and experience emotions intensely, while others may handle things with a bit more ease.

Understanding neuroticism helps us understand ourselves and others better. It can teach us to be empathetic and supportive when our friends might be feeling overwhelmed It reminds us that it's okay to have different emotional experiences because we're all unique superheroes with our own emotional powers!

As we grow older, our goals should be to lower our reactions and negative emotions. If we keep on focusing on these emotions, it could make us very sad, insecure and angry. It will feel like we are never experiencing good things in life and that everything and everyone around us is just bad.

If you lower your neuroticism, not only will you become a happier person, but people around you won't look half as bad as you thought they were before. Neuroticism plays a big role in the way we expect others to perceive us, because we never think the best of other people. If we can get rid of this superpower that causes us to be resentful and angry, we might just be able to enjoy life and the company of others.

You can slowly but surely try to get rid of neuroticism by keeping a diary of your emotions. Writing everything down is always a great idea, because once you can see everything on paper, you can analyze and solve your problems. For every negative emotion you write down, write down a positive to the situation to see the bright side. If you felt angry because a teacher corrected you in class, write it down. Next to or underneath it, you can write the positive side to the story: You now know the right answer to the question that you got wrong.

Controlling Your Neuroticism

When you're shy, it can be hard to express your feelings and communicate what you need. But with your neuroticism power, you have a super-sensitive emotional compass that guides you. You can understand and recognize your own emotions with incredible precision.

Let's say that you're feeling nervous about joining a new club at school. Your neuroticism power kicks in, and you notice those butterflies fluttering in your tummy. It's like your emotional radar is telling you, "Hey, I'm picking up some nervousness here!" This awareness can be really helpful because it allows you to acknowledge your feelings and take steps to address them.

Neuroticism can also make you incredibly empathetic. You have a unique ability to understand how others might be feeling. This makes you an excellent friend and support system for those around you. You can sense when someone is sad, worried, or excited, and you're always there to lend a helping hand or a listening ear.

Your neuroticism power also helps you pay attention to details. You notice the little things that others might miss. This means that you're great at picking up on people's emotions, body language, and subtle cues. You might notice when someone needs a friendly smile or a comforting word, making you a superhero at brightening someone's day.

Remember, being neurotic doesn't mean that there's anything wrong with you. It's just a unique part of who you are, like a colorful thread woven into the tapestry of your personality. Embracing your neuroticism can help you understand yourself better, navigate your emotions, and connect with others on a deeper level.

So, embrace your shy superhero self and use your neuroticism power to your advantage. Be the empathetic friend who notices the small details and offers support to those in need. Always remember that your emotional radar makes you special and valuable in this big world of ours!

Chapter 2: It's Not Me, It's You...Feeding the Monsters

You might be shy because your parents or guardians are shy, and you might have picked up their behavior when you were a little kid. But don't go blame them just yet! As a child, you mirror people around you, because that is the easiest way to learn. All of us are usually just younger versions of our parents or guardians at the end of the day. Despite trying your best to be a completely different version of your parents during the last few years, it is impossible to shape a completely new personality without copying and pasting some of their tricks and traits...even their quirky ones!

If your mom or dad is shy, the chances of you being shy is quite high. Being shy as a parent or guardian is not a world-ending personality trait—it's just who they are. They also have to deal with things the way you do. In fact, having a shy parent might even benefit you if you're shy. Speaking to your shy parent about shyness should be easier because they will listen and understand—or it could end up in a staring match because neither one of you knows exactly how to start a conversation like that.

The important thing is that your shy parent will understand how you feel. They might not know exactly how to help you, but they can give you tips and tricks on how they overcome shyness themselves.

Bullying Feeds the Monsters

You might have this shyness monster sitting on your shoulder because of the way kids treated you when you were younger (or how kids are still treating you). Kids can be jerks and some of them thrive off the anger and sadness they inflict on others and they do it only for a reaction.

If someone is bullying you, you need to realize the importance of letting your parents or teachers know. Your bully is a horcrux, someone who takes away the life and energy in you—you need that energy to grow and combat the problems you face, like your shyness. If someone with authority knows about your bully, they can do something about the situation, like talk to the bully or set some boundaries in place so this person can leave you alone.

Where Do You Even Start?

Combating shyness could feel like you versus the world…except you don't have a Superman to protect you, a Batman to watch over you, or the comedic relief of the Flash next to you. Where do you even start when you don't have your Justice League or any training?

Well, how do you climb a mountain? One step at a time.

It is important to understand where your shyness, or your gremlins, are from. If you can figure out where your shyness is from, either from your parents, bullying, your personality or just because you're introverted, you need to recognize that you can change it.

The first step to combat your shyness is to have awareness of it. You are probably already aware of the fact that you are shy at the back of your mind, but you need to bring that awareness into your active thoughts. You don't have to go out of your way to think about it, but when you sit in a situation where you are confronted, and your shyness takes the leading role, you need to be able to identify why you are shy.

It all starts when you are aware of the problem and can take responsibility for it. Responsibility is a big thing, especially when your current priorities include finishing your homework and making your bed in the morning. If you take responsibility for your shyness, you are the one taking the situation in your own hands.

Now, let's put it out into the universe by filling in the sentence below on a separate piece of paper, diary, or journal:

Hello, my name is _____ and I am shy because _____.

After you're done writing it down, go to the mirror or to your dog, cat, or even the plush rabbit that has been sitting on the shelf in your bedroom since you were three, and say that sentence out loud. Say it again and again and again. The only way that you can start combating your shyness is by getting the gremlin off your shoulder where you can see it.

Now that you're fully aware of it, you can take the next step to fight it. In the rest of this book, I will combat your shyness with you, giving you recipes, keys and lots of exercises. This will give you the armor and the ammunition you need to get rid of that shyness monster once and for all.

Chapter 3: Conquer your Emotions

An extrovert and an introvert walk into a room...and I bet you were expecting a joke, but the joke is on you because the introvert is probably not even in the room. The introvert is probably at home, regretting not going to a gathering, party, or event, but still content with being in bed, happily finishing a can of Pringles by themselves while watching the last season of *Star Wars, the Clone Wars*.

Not all introverts are shy, seclusion-loving vampires, but all yachts are boats and not all boats are yachts. The chances of you being introverted and shy is probably just as high as your name being Emma or Jacob...which is actually quite high, considering the fact that 1 in every 115 people are named Emma and 1 in every 222 boys are named Jacob...thanks *Twilight*.

But being shy does not just mean running away from any social interaction. It is the continuous mental exhaustion associated with overthinking. You know that feeling when you get home after a long day, and you just feel like sitting and doing nothing? That's shyness. It is shaking uncontrollably when you're confronted, and crying because someone shouted at you.

Being shy and introverted can truly be more daunting than running a marathon at times. When you are invited to go to a party, you're not just dealing with the party. You are dealing with a brain that goes fuzzy and a mouth that runs dry after "hellos" and "how are you's." You've become quite comfortable in the little corner you've made for yourself, surrounded by familiar faces and the snack bar, avoiding the over-the-top kids on the other side of the room that just make you feel like a ghost in their presence.

Shyness is probably the reason you have so many emotional insecurities. You might say, "But I know what I feel, and I am emotionally intelligent for my age; how am I emotionally insecure?"

Emotional intelligence is the ability to recognize how and what you feel. It is the ability to recognize how others feel without them telling you, even if they are not as emotionally mature as you are.

Emotional intelligence allows you to navigate and problem solve without causing friction or hatred. It's a skill, like playing guitar, or running long distances without feeling like your lungs are on fire. It is also a skill that you can practice, one that comes with age.

But if you are emotionally insecure, you are predictable. Your predictability does not mean that you are a boring person. As a matter of fact, there probably is not a boring person on this planet, except for math teachers. Jokes aside, you become predictable when you are emotionally insecure because there are telltale signs that you are shy and insecure, and people can identify it and take advantage of you.

Some of these traits include defensiveness, blame shifting, daydreaming, comparing, and invalidating. These traits together are a concoction of a very bad soup.

As a shy kid, you spend so much time in your head feeding the gremlins. You overthink and overanalyze, and through overanalyzing and overthinking, you are feeding a gremlin that should not be fed. During the 1984 movie *Gremlins*, a man receives the most adorable pet called a *mogwai*–which translates to *devil* in Chinese. The adorable creatures came with some rules: do not expose them to sunlight because sunlight can kill them, do not give them water, and do *not* feed them after midnight. If you feed your gremlin after midnight, they form a cocoon. The cocoon hatches and a very scary reptilian monster is born. This monster, a gremlin, destroys *everything*.

Your shyness is that horrible little monster, and you have to remember not to feed it. The more you feed it (with overthinking, overanalyzing and comparing yourself to others), the more it destroys.

When you sit by yourself, either during lunch, or in your room at home, you cannot help but feed this atrocious monster little bits of food when you're not meant to. Your negative thoughts and emotions regarding your insecurities, bullying, and second guessing are the crumbs of food that those pesky little creatures need when it comes to nutrition.

If you prefer spending time by yourself, you are alone with very dangerous thoughts, such as:

- Why did Sally not like me?
- Why does John not believe I can be an actor/rockstar/rapper?
- Why did I accidentally say good morning today to my teacher when it was clearly 12 pm?

This excessive worry and concern are the chocolate chip cookies that the gremlins gobble up. It sucks that these gremlins are a little hyperactive when it comes to sugar and will spend the rest of the day either burning down the files in your brain like in an episode of SpongeBob, or they will jump on a trampoline and shout more nasty things in your ear.

These gremlins love to add fuel to the fire—in this case, by forcing you to overthink all your actions. This is why you are second guessing yourself in the first place and why you feel like you perhaps don't deserve to be friends with the girls or boys you want to be friends with. It is perhaps why you feel like you are not as good as others.

There are 7 nutrients (foods) that the gremlins love to eat. The only way you can stop them is by putting them on a diet. Throw these foods out of the cupboard in your head!

The Gremlin's Favorite Diets

The first step to controlling your emotions is to throw out these pesky, expired food items that make your gremlins go all crazy. Let's go through what these foods are.

Comparing Yourself With Others

Comparing yourself with others is not a sin. It's a normal human action.

By comparing yourself to someone else, you are essentially identifying the good qualities within yourself, as well as the activities you are good at, like dancing, sports, art, or painting—you name it. Sometimes, comparing yourself happens in a split second, not because you're trying to see if you are better or worse, but to see if you are up to par with someone who is considered good at something. It is only when we compare ourselves constantly that we start to hesitate about our worth.

The problem with comparing yourself to others your age is that you are not just comparing yourself. You are also comparing yourself against what their parents have. You can't compare an apple to a 24-karat gold ring.

Unfortunately, some kids are just born into money. Think of Phoebe Buffay and Chandler Bing from the sitcom *Friends*. Often, Phoebe was short on cash and had to sleep on couches or play a guitar on the side of the road for tips. Chandler, on the other hand, had a great upbringing (or so you think) and a successful career that he hates. Despite all of it, these two opposites still find a way to be friends.

It is pretty much the same in real life (just without the laugh track). Some kids are just born with a silver spoon in hand, while others are born with a plastic fork.

It becomes pretty difficult not to compare yourself to others when you are constantly surrounded by people who have something you cannot have, and you cannot help but wonder, "Why can't I have it?" Overthinking it becomes even easier than questioning your worthiness of owning it.

In my day, I really wanted to own a GameBoy. I remember sitting at school one day with a teacher who did not want to hold class because it was the end of the school year, so she allowed all the kids to bring their toys to school. This one girl showed up in her pretty designer dress and cute little buckle shoes with a GameBoy, and I remember being completely enthralled with it.

Of course, at the time, it was probably the most wanted gaming device. A console in the palm of your hand? What more could you want?

As more and more kids started getting a GameBoy, I remember going home and begging my parents for one too, but, unfortunately, that dream never materialized. I felt like an outcast that year because I was the only kid who didn't have one. I felt like every other kid my age was laughing at me and the fact that my dad was just an electrician, and my mother was a stay-at-home mom. What I did not see though was the endless extra hours my dad worked that year to afford one of these luxurious machines for me and my sister to surprise us with at Christmas.

What your parents can or cannot afford is not supposed to dictate the way you compare yourself to others, because what your parents can afford is different to what Jimmy's parents can afford.

You should be comparing yourself to others on their talents and skills, because, in that way, you can find exactly what you're good at to focus on in the future and, perhaps, even make a career out of it.

That gremlin inside of you is trying to convince you that other kids only care for you because of your parents' money, when actually they're being just as hard on themselves as you are on yourself.

Once you can identify the fact that you are comparing yourself to others, you can be more kind to yourself. Can't throw a ball as hard as Clive in 7th grade can? So what? He probably can't outrun your opponents like you can! You can't draw a straight line or sing a high note like Becky from science can? Well, you can dance better. And it's like this with pretty much any talent. You might not have exactly the same talents and skills of someone you are envious about, but you can use that as fuel to practice, practice, practice!

With quick and easy access to social media and celebrities, it is difficult not to compare yourself to Influencers or your favorite Twitch streamer. The problem is that you do not see half of their issues and problems behind the lenses of their latest iPhones.

Comparing ourselves to others can be healthy, too, but only when you do it in a realistic way. You shouldn't compare a cake you bake at home to a cake baked by a baker who has been baking cakes for forty years—you are being completely unfair to yourself.

If you compare yourself to anyone, it should be the person you were yesterday. Today's *you* and yesterday's *you* are two completely different people. You're getting smarter and gaining more knowledge every day, and the change from yesterday and today is no different. Every day in school, from your friends, and through your own experiences, you're learning new things. You're becoming wiser and better at solving problems and making smart choices.

You're also becoming a stronger person. You face challenges, try new things, and step out of your comfort zone. This helps you grow as a person and become more confident and resilient. You're like a superhero of personal growth, always pushing yourself to be better. And the way you step out of your comfort zone with challenges and things you enjoy should be replicated with your shyness. If you want to try a new sport, you have to go through trial and error, and sometimes you fail. Combatting your shyness is much the same.

As you discover more about who you are, what you love, and what makes you unique, you're getting to know yourself on a deeper level. Understanding your strengths, interests, and values helps you make choices that make you truly happy. You're becoming a master at being yourself! As you master yourself, you become more self-aware, and this self-awareness is the exact tool that will help you fight off unwanted shyness-gremlins.

Life can throw curveballs, but guess what? You're becoming a master at bouncing back! You're learning how to handle challenges, adapt to new situations, and find creative solutions. You're an expert problem-solver, always ready to save the day.

If you compare yourself to the person that you were yesterday, you're learning to see the good in every day, and you are learning to see the good in yourself. You can appreciate the small things, you can be mindful of the present moment, and you can find joy in everyday adventures, because you were a little bit dumber, less kind, and harder on yourself yesterday, but today, you're looking forward to the person you can be tomorrow.

Let's Make a Pizza to Stop You From Comparing Yourself to Others

Imagine that you're on a delicious pizza adventure, but instead of enjoying your own unique pizza, you start comparing it to everyone else's slices. Your friend's pizza might have extra toppings, and your classmate's pizza might look perfectly round. It's easy to start feeling like your own pizza isn't as cool or tasty.

But here's the secret: Your pizza is special, just like you! It has its own flavors, toppings, and crust that make it uniquely delicious. So, let's learn how to savor our own pizza without comparing it to others.

First, sprinkle some gratitude seasoning on your pizza. Take a moment to appreciate the awesome things in your life—your loving family, supportive friends, or even your favorite hobbies. When you focus on what makes you happy, it's easier to see the toppings on your own pizza and enjoy them.

Next, let's top your pizza with realistic goals. Imagine adding your favorite toppings, like becoming a great soccer player or learning to play a musical instrument. These goals should be based on your own interests and abilities, not on what others are doing. Remember, your pizza adventure is about your own journey; it's not a race with others.

Now, sprinkle some kindness Parmesan on top. Instead of being hard on yourself, practice self-love and acceptance. Give yourself a big slice of kindness and remind yourself that you're amazing just the way you are. Embrace your quirks, talents, and imperfections—they make your pizza extra special!

Practicing self-love is almost as important as the base of a pizza, but that doesn't mean that you can't improve the recipe. You always need to be on the lookout for a better recipe, ways to improve and better yourself so that you can grow and become a better person. At the same time, you should remember that even if you don't grow as fast as you want or as quickly as someone else, that you grow and improve at your own pace. You should always love yourself, because if you don't, it will be a lot more difficult to take on challenges and love others.

To make your pizza party even more fun, invite positive friends to join you. Surround yourself with people who appreciate and support you for who you are. Just like different pizza flavors, friends come in all shapes and sizes. Together, you can celebrate each other's unique pizzas and enjoy the party!

Lastly, take a mindful bite of your pizza. Chew slowly, so you can savor the flavors; feel and taste everything: the cheese, the dough, the toppings, and the spices. Whenever you catch yourself comparing your pizza to others, gently remind yourself to focus on your own pizza adventure. Pay attention to the cheesy goodness in your slice and the exciting toppings that you've chosen for yourself.

Remember, life is like a pizza party, and you have the tastiest slice! Embrace your own flavors, set goals that make you happy, sprinkle kindness on yourself, and surround yourself with positive, pizza-loving friends. By doing this, you'll savor every bite of your own unique pizza adventure and stop comparing it to others. Enjoy the journey, my pizza-loving friend!

Overanalyzing

There is absolutely nothing worse than coming home after a long day, and all you can think about is that one very silly moment when you asked your teacher if you could go "know your blows" in the bathroom quickly.

Luckily for you, your teacher did not seem to catch on, but your fellow classmates were snickering at you for the rest of the day. Even something as silly as someone else mispronouncing your own name can cause a type of shame and discomfort that could potentially be more painful than stepping on a Lego block.

Another part of shyness that no one talks about, is what if you said something wrong? Or, what if you didn't say something wrong, but your friend is mad, and now it *feels* like you said something wrong?

Feeling insecure about what you do and say is not a nice feeling, and it plays a big part in stopping you from doing anything in the future. If you fell down a flight of stairs once because you were running, would you do it again? Probably, but if it happens a second time, you would probably be more careful. Your brain is more careful around situations that felt uncomfortable before, ensuring that you do not feel that horrendous feeling again. Our gremlin, on the other hand, is bashfully enjoying handfuls of your insecurity to fill up its belly and becoming even more rowdy to make sure that you never socialize or talk ever again.

Be the Detective

Imagine being a super-detective with an incredible mind that loves to solve mysteries. However, sometimes, your detective skills can go into overdrive, and you find yourself overanalyzing everything like a never-ending puzzle. Don't worry, young sleuth! Here are some fun tips to help you put those overanalyzing thoughts to rest.

First, imagine your brain as a magnifying glass. Just like a detective zooms in on clues, your mind likes to zoom in on thoughts. But remember, a magnifying glass makes things look bigger than they are in real life. So, when your thoughts start getting too big, imagine yourself shrinking that magnifying glass and turning it into a fun toy. Let your mind play with other thoughts and let go of the ones that make you overthink.

Next, go on a "brain break" adventure! Sometimes, your mind can get tired from all the thinking. So, it's important to give it a break and go on a mini-adventure. Take a walk in nature, play a game, or engage in a hobby that you enjoy. Let your brain relax and have some fun. This helps your mind reset and prevents it from going into overdrive.

You can also create a "worry jar" for your thoughts. Imagine having a magical jar that can hold all your over-analyzing thoughts. Whenever you catch yourself overthinking, write down your thoughts on a piece of paper and put them in the jar. You can even decorate the jar with stickers to make it extra special. This way, you're acknowledging your thoughts but also letting them go. It's like capturing butterflies and releasing them back into the wild!

Another fun strategy is to practice "detective distraction." When your mind starts overanalyzing, distract it with something enjoyable. Engage in activities that capture your attention and bring you joy. It could be reading a thrilling book, solving puzzles, or dancing to your favorite tunes. By focusing on something fun, you redirect your mind's energy and give it a break from overthinking.

Embrace the "mystery of uncertainty." Life is full of unknowns, just like a thrilling mystery novel. Instead of trying to solve every uncertainty, learn to embrace the excitement of not knowing everything. Remember, some of the best surprises and adventures come from embracing the unknown and going with the flow. So, put on your detective hat and enjoy the twists and turns that life brings.

Lastly, talk to a trusty sidekick. Every detective needs a sidekick to share their thoughts and feelings. Talk to a trusted friend, family member, or even a caring teacher about your overanalyzing tendencies. They can provide a fresh perspective and help you see things from a different angle. Plus, solving mysteries together is always more fun!

So, dear detective, it's great to use your analytical mind, but overanalyzing can be exhausting. Shrink that magnifying glass, embark on exciting adventures, distract your mind, embrace uncertainty, and lean on your trusty sidekicks. By doing so, you'll find a better balance between solving mysteries and enjoying the mysteries of life itself. Happy sleuthing!

Criticism Is Your Mortal Enemy

There is nothing worse than hearing someone rip into your efforts when you feel like it was your best effort yet.

When you are introverted, you spend a lot more time in your head making up conversations than you do conversing with people. This causes your head to become a safe space for your thoughts and yourself. You don't have to step out of your comfort zone when all you have to deal with is the voice in your head.

Because we spend so much time with our inner monologues and comparing ourselves to others, we become exceptionally critical of our own work. The voice in our head starts being mean, instead of telling you what to do and what not to do.

Sometimes, others criticize us and "confirm" what the voice inside of our heads has been saying the whole time. This can cause feelings of failure, hopelessness, and self-doubt to elevate. Our inner critics stop us from doing things we enjoy because they make us believe that we are not good at them or make us believe that we won't succeed. We try to reassure our inner critic, focusing on the opinions other people have of us, and when it matches up with what our inner critic has to say, we often give up or stop trying.

Pretend you are building a papier mâché house. You have spent hours and hours on this house, trying to carve and paste the perfect little walls, roof, and doors. You even left open space for the windows and doors to be slipped into the frame. You've thought of everything, adding a fancy hinge to make the roof lift up so you can decorate the inside with easy access. You are quite pleased with your handiwork because it really looks good. It is sleek and pretty and...and then it's not anymore.

The more you look at it, the more you notice the uneven paintwork because the papier mâché underneath is not smooth. Then you see that the glue did not dry in certain places you painted over, which means the paper got wet, and now it is peeling off.

Negative self-criticism is your worst enemy. The negative self-criticism is telling you that you could have built a better house. Building a better house is not necessarily a bad thing, because it is always good to measure yourself up against yourself, but it is also a way that you can continuously put pressure on yourself that you don't need.

Negative self-criticism places a lot of unnecessary stress and hurt in your life, making it difficult to talk to yourself, respect yourself, and see the negative self-criticism, which causes us to feel less productive and less successful, and it can make us feel insecure. Studies have shown that negative self-criticism will slow you down from reaching your goals by crushing motivation.

Unfortunately, self-criticism does not always come from a place in our hearts; it can come from the hearts around us. We see our parents or siblings criticize themselves and others, and that becomes such a regular part of life that it ends up wiggling its way into our heads.

How do we turn down the volume of the self-critic yapping on in our heads?

How to Take Criticism

Taking criticism is difficult, not just from yourself, but from others, too. The difficult part is that criticism brings out the vulnerability in you, the things that you are insecure about. Self-criticism often focuses on all of the activities you are bad at and all your negative characteristics, and it ignores your talents and good characteristics.

The antidote to negative self-criticism is to be compassionate with yourself. Self-compassion is when you replace that very mean, critical police officer in your head that catches you in every bad moment.

Think of the day when you were practicing a sport in school (it could have been any sport: hockey, football, basketball, you name it), and you keep on messing up. A negative coach would have shouted at you or even kicked you off the field or court, but a good, positive coach would have pulled you aside and told you that you are doing your best and that you have grown. The positive coach would also express your faults, but he or she would explain how to fix them.

Think of replacing the negative voice in your head with a positive coach. In order for you to start easing the pain of self-criticism, you need to be able to say these kinds of reassuring things to yourself.

Positive Affirmations

There are a few things you can say to yourself to combat the negative self-criticism. Some of these phrases include:

- "You are doing your best."
- "You are doing better than you think."
- "You are doing a good job."
- "You are a talented person."

Change "Should" With "Could"

"Should" is such a negative word, because it makes you think of what you would have done instead of what you can do. If you replace "should" with "could" in your vocabulary, you are creating a positive scenario for yourself by assuring yourself that you can do it in the future. You are also taking that next grown-up step to admit what went wrong and how you can fix it.

Say, for instance, you did not study for a test and received a bad grade because you thought you knew the material. Instead of saying, "I should have studied. I should not have spent all my time on TikTok," say, "I could have studied more, but I procrastinated."

Here, you identify what you did to cause the bad grades but also identify how to fix it. In this case, it would be better time management and self-control.

Question the Negative Statement

Sometimes, negative, critical thoughts are quite unnecessarily harsh and cruel. They can even be illogical and incorrect, too. Your negative voice is a bully, and you should think of it as one.

If your inner voice ever bullies you, ask it, "Why?" Why do you think that you are not talented enough to audition for the talent show? You have practiced the song you want to sing, you have been singing for a long time, and you feel happy when you do it, so why would it be a bad idea to audition?

This technique of battling your inner voice is very effective, especially when you write it down. An example of using this technique would look like this:

Thought: "I am going to fail tomorrow's test."

Q: "Why am I going to fail the test? Are there any tests I have failed before that cause me to feel like this?"

A: "I passed biology two weeks ago, I studied the work, and I am a good student. As long as I don't leave it to the last day, I can ace this thing!"

When you write down the argument to the statements of your negative self-criticism, you quickly realize that your worry isn't required.

You'll be fine! Your inner monologue is just being mean to yourself.

Take Away the Power From the Voice in Your Head

If the inner critic is talking way too much in your head, and he doesn't want to go away, don't shoo him away. Invite him in for coffee, tea, and cake—but make sure to give him a silly voice. Imagine the critic in your head being Dr. Doofenshmirtz or the Earl from Lemongrab…how can you take the voice seriously if it sounds silly?

Reduce Your Expectations

The biggest flaw we sometimes have is expecting a lot from ourselves and a lot from the people around us. Because we strive for perfection, we often force ourselves to believe that what we are doing is not good enough, and that is simply not true.

Recognize that you have expectations of yourself to be perfect, and because you are human, you cannot be perfect or do things perfectly. You are going to make mistakes. You are going to experience challenges. If you stop expecting yourself to be perfect and allow yourself to grow and improve, you are going to have a more positive experience with the voice in your head.

This is where positive affirmations come in. It is important to tell yourself what you are good at and what you are not. This can guide you to better yourself to reach the expectations you have.

Some examples of positive affirmations include:

- I am strong and brave, no matter what comes my way.
- I can handle anything.
- Every day I am stronger, wiser, and happier.
- The shyness monster has no power over me!

Difficulty Trusting Others

You have been rejected by your peers for not having the latest iPhone (you obviously have a PearPhone instead) or lunch money to go buy McDonalds fries, and now, you're feeling particularly fragile, like Woody being left behind by a grown-up Andy.

Your gremlins are giggling in your chest now as we speak, because they are getting what they want. They cornered you in a fragile position where you are malleable like hot metal.

How to Trust People

Imagine that you're on a treasure hunt, seeking the most valuable treasure of all—trust! But just like a treasure hunt, finding trust can be not only an exciting adventure, but also a challenge that might make you feel hopeless at times. However, like in every Indiana Jones movie, there is always some kind of clue and some kind of map to find the treasure. Let's start with finding that first.

Imagine trust being a key to open the archives to the great hall where we keep more trust. It unlocks the door to wonderful friendships and connections, but only when you're ready for it and only when you want to embark on the journey. To find this key, you must be open to new experiences. Just like exploring hidden caves and secret passages, be willing to step out of your comfort zone and meet new people. You never know what amazing friendships might be waiting to be discovered!

Next, picture trust as a puzzle. Each person you meet is like a unique puzzle piece that builds who you are as a person. Some pieces might fit perfectly with your puzzle, while others might not. Take your time getting to know people and let them share their stories and interests. Piece by piece, you'll start forming a beautiful, trust-filled picture.

Now, imagine trust as a recipe for a delicious friendship cake. Every friendship needs a mix of ingredients, like honesty, kindness, and understanding. Share your thoughts and feelings, and encourage them to do the same. As you mix these ingredients together, you'll create a strong foundation of trust.

Trust is like a bridge connecting people's hearts. Imagine yourself as a master bridge-builder, constructing trust bridges wherever you go. Start by being trustworthy yourself. Keep your promises, be reliable, and respect others' feelings. Soon enough, you'll find people walking across the trust bridges you've built, and they'll be eager to build their own bridges with you.

Lastly, think of trust as a garden that grows over time. Just like planting seeds and tending to them, trust needs patience and care. Nurture your friendships by listening attentively, offering support, and being there when they need you. Water your friendships with kindness and watch them bloom into trust-filled trees.

So, embrace the puzzle pieces, mix the friendship cake ingredients, build trust bridges, and tend to your trust garden. As you embark on this exciting journey, you'll discover that trusting others can lead to amazing friendships and unforgettable experiences.

Trust is Earned

You do not have to trust everyone. Trust has always been something that is earned, not something that is handed out like free samples. The sooner you realize that you do not have to trust everyone, the happier you will be—and the less anxious and nervous you will be. It's okay to trust people, too, like the friend who listens to you and the sister or brother who was there for you when you felt your parents or guardian weren't. But if you feel like you trust people too quickly or that people use you because they misuse trust, you don't have to trust them.

Our trust comes from our caregivers, parents, guardians, or teachers who look after us as children. As kids, we rely on our caregivers to show us the difference between good and bad, right and wrong, but they also show us the difference between willingness and unwillingness. They show us the difference between doing and saying. We are all human, and we all make mistakes, and our caregivers and parents are not excluded. Sometimes, parents make mistakes and break promises, like forgetting to play Barbie with you after work. A small incident like that could lead to a lifelong problem with trust.

As we become older, we are less trusting, not only because of the damage already done by our caregivers and parents for not following through and meeting the needs that we require, but also because of other bad experiences with trust in school or friends.

Now, this book is not a place to lecture you on your childhood trauma, but it is here to tell you that it is okay not to trust people because of your past or because someone hurt you, and you have a valid reason not to trust someone.

You can set firm boundaries with people you do not trust after they have broken your trust. It sucks that you have to trust someone first before setting boundaries, but this will teach you what to do in the future. Setting boundaries helps you gain the trust of people who deserve it, but it also helps to guide you through difficult situations where you need to decide between good and bad actions.

You can also trust someone slowly. You can wait for someone to prove to you that they are trustworthy. It is difficult to determine if someone is trustworthy at the beginning of any friendship, but there are a few qualities they have that will give you some peace as to why you can trust them.

If you make a new friend, and they are consistent, they can be trustworthy. Being consistent means that they are not like a jack-in-the-box; they won't freak out at random times, they will always be there for you, and they will always treat you the same as you treat them. A trustworthy person is also compassionate. A new friend who cares about you and other people could potentially be a very trustworthy friend.

A friend that is trustworthy will be calm and respectable around you. They will treat you as an equal with no expectations and will be patient with you. They will also come across as a calm person. They might even make you feel calm!

A trustworthy friend is also a friend who learns who you are. They will go out of their way to learn about the things you like, which could be a book series or the characters of a sitcom.

Trusting someone is difficult, but once you can determine who is trustworthy and what boundaries you have, you can feel a bit more relaxed about trusting just anyone.

My Parents are Feeding the Gremlins...Help!

Often, we find that our loving and accepting parents like putting us in boxes, not because they want to, but perhaps because it is comforting to put kids in a box. I mean, we box cats and dogs into categories: cats are lazy and mean and dogs are always friendly and begging for food under the table. It is comfortable to be able to know exactly what to expect from someone.

Putting someone in a box is easy because you know what to expect. This is why we, and our parents, are often guilty of putting others in boxes. Your parents want to put you in a box not to belittle you or to bring you down, but they actually do it because 1) they care and 2) that was the way they were raised.

Your Parents Can Help You Out of the Box

Talking to your parents is going to be a process—like baking a cake from scratch.

First, you need to make sure you have all the ingredients and the recipe to make the cake.

How to Talk to Parents
20 minutes, 3 ingredients

Ingredients:

- 1-4 parents/guardians, depending on the situation
- 1 child (you)
- Paper (optional)
- Pen (optional)

Directions:

1. Try to figure out exactly what you want to ask or tell your parents in your own time. Make sure that you are communicating clearly and that your thoughts are well thought out and structured in such a way that they understand. Often, we think that our thoughts make sense, but it only makes sense to us and not to others. A good way to figure out what you are going to say is by writing down exactly how you feel (that's where the pen and paper come in).

2. Once you know what you are going to say, practice in the mirror (or to your dog). By practicing what you will say, you are subconsciously working through the speech that you are going to give your parents, ironing out all the kinks.

3. Make sure that your parents are relaxed and have time to sit and chat. Sometimes, parents are a little bit stressed and under pressure. Imagine that they have to hand in a very big project tomorrow, except that

they have a big project every day. That's exactly what work is. Maybe a weekend is a bit better for your parents, or even an hour or two after dinner when they are relaxing and not cleaning the kitchen.

You have your speech ready, and your parents or guardians are having a nice relaxing evening…now what?

Backing away after coming this far is not an option, but your heart just cannot seem to accept the fact that you have to talk to them. Suddenly, a person you have been talking to your whole life feels strange and it feels like your entire body is on fire.

How do you even start telling them how you feel? Telling people how you feel is one thing, asking them to stop something is another thing…and this is where you identify the fact that you have been feeding this gremlin food and lots of it. This gremlin deserves no food.

4. Take a deep breath, go over your notes and start off slow. Start with the easy part of

talking to your parents: describing the way you feel.

One part of being shy is living too much inside your head. You become too self-conscious to what other people are saying, and the thing is, your parents are not other people. Your parents are the people who stand behind you, supporting every crazy thing that comes out of your mouth.

5. Try to think of their reaction. Chances are that your parents will react in a way you expect them to and will understand you. They want you to be comfortable, and they will make an active effort. The worst thing that can happen is they might tell you something like "you will grow out of it," but if you repeat the conversation another time to show that it is important to you, they will eventually understand. Sometimes, it takes a bit of work to allow others to understand you and how you feel.

If you really cannot get a single word out, it is a good idea to slip a letter underneath their door (another handy-dandy trick for the pen and paper) and wait. They will come talk to you themselves.

Chapter 4: Mindset

Many things can change when you put your mind to it, but miracles aren't going to happen out of the blue. Think of the Wright Brothers: They wanted to fly, but they definitely weren't going to do it by flapping their arms and jumping up and down. Instead, they worked hard and assembled a machine with wings to make their dreams come true!

Your mindset is the voice in your head whispering to you as you go about your day. That voice can determine how you view the world, your opinions, the habits you develop and break, and even how you react in situations of happiness and stress. Your mindset is such a big part of your life that it can determine if you will be successful or not. Think of it as the narrator before a Dr. Seuss movie starts—it sets the tone for who you are, how your day will go, and even sometimes how you perceive and treat other people.

Often, our mindsets, or these voices in our heads, hold us back from doing things we really wish we could do. We wish to be astronauts, firefighters, doctors, lawyers and rockstars. Our mindsets sometimes bully us to make us believe that we are untalented, stupid, shy, and boring. Our mindsets sometimes force our focus on others, because there is always someone else out there on social media who can do exactly what we want to do, but even better.

We often see things in a negative way instead of in a positive light, almost as if we are preparing ourselves for disappointment. But who said that we were going to be disappointed? Unless you did not study for your test today, there is no real reason to expect failure. This negativity whispering in our ears day in and day out keeps us from trying things, speaking to people, and making a difference.

You also cannot blame other people for your mindset, because no one else tells you what you should think—only you tell yourself what to think. Changing your mindset starts with you recognizing that you are negative in situations that probably are not the worst in the world.

It is not consoling at all to hear that your problems are not big, especially since they are quite big to you, and sometimes it feels like your world is flooding because of them. You just have to realize that the people you are expressing your problems to also have problems that they are worrying about.

Being negative in general is a way to defend yourself. You are protecting yourself against the worst that could possibly happen, almost as if you expect every outcome to be the worst. Sometimes, it is good to protect yourself against bad things, but other times, it's just counterintuitive. It's almost like you want to stop yourself from being successful or famous or happy.

Unfortunately, preparing for the worst is quite a natural reaction. Our ape-like ancestors had to prepare for extremely bad things to happen all the time, including death and even attacks by big, scary predators. Today, we don't have big, scary monsters finding us in the dark around the corner to chew us up for dinner. We only have ourselves to blame for the negativity we materialize by believing it.

Mind Over Matter

Every day starts with mindset.

If you get up in the morning and believe that you are going to have a bad day, the chances are high that you will have a bad day because you will subconsciously manifest your thoughts. When you are excited for something, either watching Taylor Swift live or playing Minecraft with your friends, you believe that you're going to have a good day.

Once upon a time, what we would consider a crazy man hiked up El Capitan in Yosemite National Park without any gear. Alex Hannold climbed all the way up a mountain with no climbing gear and no rope. He trusted himself. He *believed* in himself.

Another similarly crazy man, Wim Hof, took himself up Kilimanjaro with nothing but a pair of shorts and some shoes—not even a cup of coffee or a jacket. Wim is not just a crazy mountain man, but he's a crazy swimmer, too, holding the world record for the longest swim under ice...188 feet (57.5 meters). How?

No one is following your every move, commenting on what you are doing, the quality of your life or who you are. Would you criticize and comment on your best friend, mom, or cat the way you are criticizing and breaking yourself down daily?

You might ask, "How do I change my mindset? How do I become more positive? It feels like I have been like this since the day I was born."

Let's follow the advice of the great Emperor Palpatine: "Do it. Just do it, darn it."

Let's Change Your Mindset

Stop Focusing on Negative Thoughts

Good and bad things happen all the time to all kinds of people. Remember how Doctor Doofenshmirtz somehow gets his *-inator* blown up because he has bad intentions, and Phineas and Ferb never get in trouble for building naughty things because they had good intentions.

Bad and good things almost happen at random, unless it was something you were avoiding subconsciously like the fact that you did not study for your math exam. I am talking about not studying for a test and then failing it—you know what I am talking about!

Professor Allison Ledgerwood, who describes herself as a professional people watcher (a social psychologist), conducted an experiment with a group of people at her university (TEDx Talks, 2013). In this experiment, she had two groups who were assigned the exact same operation to cure and treat a very bad disease. The operation would include a special implant that would give you X-Ray vision.

To Group 1, she described this essential operation as 70% successful and to Group 2, she described it as 30% failure. Group 1 was more inclined to like the surgery. I mean, who doesn't want x-ray vision to see when mom walks past your bedroom door so you can hide your phone when you're supposed to be in bed?

But if you think about it, the surgical outcome is exactly the same.

She then continued by telling Group 1 that the operation has a 30% chance of failure. Surprisingly, Group 1 changed their tunes exceptionally fast, deciding that the X-ray vision was not worth it. Group 2 was told that the operation has a 70% success rate, but they still didn't budge.

The experiment puts a perspective on negative thoughts. Once you start to realize that there is a chance of failure or a chance of something bad happening, you tend to think about it more. But when you think about positive things first, about the fact that we have a 70% chance of success, we tend to be more focused on the positives.

Negative thoughts linger regardless of the situation. It is almost like gum stuck to the bottom of your shoe: it doesn't go anywhere.

Humans focus on negative things far more than positive things. Once something negative crawls into your brain, it's almost like a bear finding a comfy cave in winter: It just sleeps there.

Unfortunately, there is no magic switch in our brains that fixes our mindsets. We have to take accountability for the fact that we think negatively. You can change your mindset, but it will take some effort.

Replace Your Negative Thoughts With Positive Ones

Being negative is like bumping your toe on the corner of the coffee table. Is it sore? Yes. Is it inconvenient? Extremely. Does it make your day better? Definitely not! Is it worth saying ugly words about? No, because the lecture that mom and dad give you will not make the toe you stubbed feel any better.

Think of negative thoughts like saying bad words out loud when you know you're not allowed to. Not only does saying bad words get you into trouble, but it does not make your toe feel any better. Negative thoughts will not make you feel better, either. They just are what they are: bad.

We can always try to replace these bad thoughts with something more positive or something completely off topic. It's like replacing swear words with "snickerdoodle" and "jumpin' jiminy." I mean, who doesn't like a snickerdoodle?

In 2005, scientists conducted an experiment to prove that mindset has a lot more power than you'd expect. During the study, a group of people were told that they would be inflicted with mild pain, like stubbing your toe on the edge of the coffee table. Instead of exposing these individuals to mild pain, the scientists actually exposed them to severe pain–pain equivalent to burning your skin. The group's pain rating was reported to be a lot lower than the severe pain they were exposed to.

This study shows that your mindset can determine the way you experience things. The people exposed to severe pain in this study expected mild pain, but because they anticipated the pain, it was almost like they could prepare for it. Think of when people get piercings: Other than the fact that they are paying for pain, the piercer tells them when they are going to punch the holes through their ears. Many of these individuals say that the pain is not bad at all, but is that true, or is it the fact that they have prepared their mindset to experience pain?

You can change and mold your mindset in the same way.

Every time you think a bad thought, like "I am going to fail because I am going to stumble over my words," or "People don't like me because they think I'm weird," try to find a quality in yourself that is positive. Instead, tell yourself that you will make it, and that you might not have done your best, but that you tried.

We are the only ones who can combat these emotions and negative thoughts. There is no such thing as a mindset police; not even your mom knows what is going on in your head. You are the sole custodian to the key of the door to your head. You are the only person who can change how you feel or think, and you are the only person who can tell other people how you feel and think.

List Things You Are Grateful For

We are so used to constantly being negative, constantly being sad, and always seeing the bad things in others and ourselves, that when we actively sit down and write the things that we are grateful for and the things that are good in our lives, we might just be able to kick out the little devil sitting on our shoulder whispering negativity into our ears.

A common misconception is that we will feel better if we talk about all the negative occurrences in our lives, like if we had a bad day or experienced bad emotions like vulnerability, anger, or insecurity from shyness. By bringing this baggage home with you, you are bringing all your negative emotions into your world, despite trying to protect your world from the one outside. We always talk about how bad our day was, how we accidentally messed up something that we didn't mean to, and how one person is bringing us down at school. We never talk about how the teacher helped us understand a challenging math concept or how our friend shared their desserts with us.

In this instance, bad emotions and bad feelings can be compared to a cold or flu. Often, you pick up a cold at school from a kid in your class, a teacher, or anyone you come into contact with. The problem with a cold or flu is that in the first few days of being infected, you don't know that you're sick. You carry on with your life normally, taking that bacteria or virus home with you without knowing it.

After a few days, your mom or sister might become sick—and you might even be sick, too.

Negative emotions act in the same way. You bring them home in the form of a bad mood or being oversensitive. This is essentially the virus or bacteria that infected you—the bullying or bad emotions. Then, when you go home and take it out on your family and close friends, like shouting at them to leave you alone or hiding in your room, you are infecting them with bad moods and emotions, too. If you take all these bad emotions home and infect the people around you, you will feel even more alone.

The fact is that you are focusing on these bad emotions. It has become your mindset, controlling your day and how you treat others and yourself.

By shifting your mindset from a negative to a positive, you will be able to take control of your day. You will be able to take control of how you feel. You will also be able to distinguish between your safe space—which is home—and school.

One way you can get rid of this negative mindset is by starting a journal. Don't jot down only all the bad emotions that you have, even though it is a great idea to get all of it out, make sure to write down all the good things too. Examples include that you have friends, that you have a roof over your head, and that you have eyes to see the world with. Many others in the world aren't so lucky.

Write down your list as soon as you get home. Always remind yourself that you are surrounded by a family and people that love you and that you are talented, smart, or creative. Once you think of the good things in your life, the one small inconvenience that made you feel like your day was ruined a few hours ago seems like nonsense!

Seven Mindsets

Seven voices in my head?! (Insert shocked cat meme here). How can you focus with seven different voices in your head? You're probably thinking that your head is already loud with this one gremlin talking your ears off, never mind seven others. But there are not seven voices in your head—there are seven different tones and focuses to the voice in your head. It is the way these voices are trained.

Think of it like singing: You get different types of singing in different places of your mouth and sinus cavities—head voice, chest voice, and whatever Mariah Carey does. Your mind can be trained, and if you put some time and effort into it, you can become a completely different person.

The Seven Mindsets was a theory developed by a group of scientists who wanted answers to the same questions: What is the difference between happy and unhappy people, and what do these happy people all have in common? It turns out that they all have very loud heads, but that they can train them.

These are these seven mindsets:

- Everything is possible
- Passion first
- We are connected
- Attitude of gratitude
- 100% accountable

- Live to give
- The time is now

We are not going to explore every single mindset of the seven, but there are some important ones that can really help you recognize the power within your heart. We are going to explore the ones that will make you feel like Superman when he came to earth–indestructible!

Everything is Possible

Your big dreams can come true.

Think about it: The cellphone you use to call your mom to pick you up or the book that you're reading right now was once someone's great, big dream. At some point, someone woke up with the idea of creating a phone or a book, and they made it happen. With creativity, passion, and a willingness to work, you can make anything happen!

If your goal, for now, is to make more friends, you first have to realize that it is possible. It might seem like a lot of work that you have to put in because you're not just working to make friends, you're working through your shyness, and you are working through your own shortcomings, and that is such a big step to make. If you're sitting in class quietly, think to yourself, what am I doing now to make this happen? How am I making friends? These questions should follow you around as you go about your day, because the more you think about it and work on it, the greater the chances are for it to happen.

100% Accountable

You are not the non-player character (NPC) in your life. You are the main character. You make the quests happen. You run the whole show!

Why sit back and watch your life rush past you as other people make decisions and force you into a box? You should take that box and tear it, pushing past your limits. You should always be looking for a way to better yourself, and to push yourself emotionally, physically, and mentally. If you continue pushing yourself, growing, and becoming stronger, it is much easier to follow your big dreams.

If you try to talk to someone different every single day, you would have spoken to at least twenty new people a month (weekends excluded). By the fifteenth person, it should feel like spreading butter on toast—easy, natural, and rewarding! But you should not stop there; you should push even more—join that photography club, that school band, or that play! With all the hard work you have put in, you deserve some recognition.

Chapter 5: You Are Wasting Your Time Being Shy

No one cares about you.

No, I am not saying that no one cares about you literally and that your parents are going to drop you off in front of the Dursley's doorstep and forget about you. There are a lot of people in your life who love and adore you that care very much.

However, I am saying that sometimes we forget that we are the NPCs in other people's lives and that our class friends, acquaintances, and teachers do not notice anything about us enough to care about it.

Think about it like this: You wake up and spend time with yourself. You think to yourself, speak to yourself, feed yourself. In your world, you are the main character of the glorious six book series. Everyone in school feels exactly the same: They have to deal with themselves every day. In your life, your friends only exist when they are in your field of vision, and the moment they step away, they disappear from your main memory (your Random Access Memory, or RAM), almost like how a character disappears in a video game until they appear on the screen again. Technically, they are no longer a part of your game, and you forget about them (for the moment). When they come back, their character is loaded back into your screen and back into your memory.

The same way you feel about your friends is the way they feel about you. The way you feel about yourself is the way they feel about themselves.

Say you find yourself in a situation where you accidentally say "poop" instead of "droop" (in whichever multiverse that would be), and you feel embarrassed and haunted by the slip of your tongue. To your friends, that is one second's humor before they carry on worrying about themselves again. They will not remember what you did.

You have to remember that everyone else is so busy living their lives that they don't really take notes on yours. Did you accidentally trip on September 22 and bump your nose on the wall in front of your crush? They don't remember.

I'm definitely sure they can't even remember what they had for dinner a few days ago, either. Did you accidentally drift so far off into daydream land when you were in math that you couldn't hear the teacher shout your name in front of 30 other kids?

It might be embarrassing and scary in that moment, but you have to remember that two minutes from now, no one will remember what you did because they are back in their own world, worrying about their own things. I like to call this phenomenon "first person syndrome."

Stop Writing Other People's Stories for Them

When you are busy in your head writing your own story, you might find yourself creating a new narrative for your friends. You place them in a certain box or category so that when you decide to do something out of your comfort zone, their reaction matches up to the expectation you have of them. Often, these expectations are negative, for example, you picture them laughing at you, bullying you, or being mean. Half of the time, these other kids don't even think of you in any other way than being a classmate.

As humans, we are hypocrites, and we need to admit it. We always ask people nicely not to judge us or expect things from us, but how can you ask that if you are creating expectations of them in your head?

The moment you realize that other people don't really pay that much attention to you is the moment you will be able to play guitar for your school recital.

The way I learned about first-person syndrome was during my first performance at music school—a showcase night. I had played guitar for exactly one year. I had begged for years to start music lessons because I wanted to be the next Kirk Hammett. I wanted to impress my dad, because when he didn't nap on the couch ignoring his family, he was listening to Metallica.

When I was 14, my parents finally said that I could attend music class for the first time. The lessons were one-on-one, perfect for first-time learners. If I made a mistake, it was only between me and my music teacher. No one outside the walls of his classroom would know about my mistakes.

I was invited to be a part of my teacher's student showcase night–a night where all his students played in front of their parents to showcase the talents they were building on. Two weeks before the show, my teacher decided (on a whim) that I had to play a duet with a girl that I had never met before. The fact that I had never met her was not as bothersome, because at that point, I had become very cocky about my great beginner skills. I had put so much time and effort into rehearsing guitar that it became my life.

I practiced for days on end to make sure that I had my part of the song down, following my mom into the bathroom when she showered to play her the song, and taking my guitar in the car with me to the supermarket. My guitar (and that song) was basically an extension of my body and mind.

During the evening of the show, I met with another group of musicians, all of whom had had lessons since elementary school. All of them had practiced longer hours, had more years of experience, and had better equipment, so they were all better than me in my head. I was scared that I might look like an idiot in comparison, that I might be horrible on stage, and that I might mess up.

When I got on stage to play my song, I felt like the world would end. I was making mistakes, losing tempo, and it was all I could think about until I ended the song. I stormed off and hid in the hallway when I was done with my performance, disappointed. In my head, I was so focused on the notes that I played wrong, on the tempo I had lost, and on the mistakes that I made.

After a few minutes alone, my dad sat down next to me in the quiet hallway, then he said something profound.

"You might have noticed your mistakes because you made them, but I can promise you that no one else noticed them nearly as much. They all thought that you were amazing because that was something they could not do. Something they would never do. They would never get up on the stage and play through the entire song after one mistake. Every person in that hall would've left when they made their first mistake, but you powered through and played until the very end."

That night, I realized that I was so focused on pleasing the crowd and being perfect that I didn't even think about the good job that I was doing and about how hard I had practiced for my performance. I should have been kinder to myself and to my performance, even though I made mistakes. I learned from that that I should not put my ideas into other people's heads, because what they are thinking is not what I was thinking.

The crowd of parents probably did not even think about my mistakes after my performance, but rather remembered my performance as a whole. I was just writing their characters without knowing who they really are and what I thought they would think based on what I was thinking of myself.

Chapter 6: Get Better Everyday

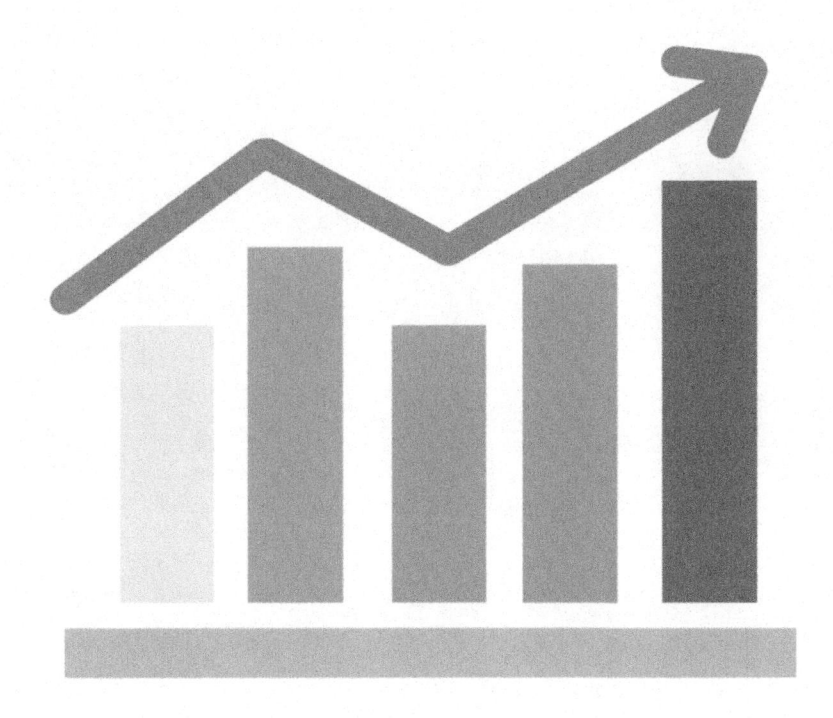

It is important to reward effort when you step out of your comfort zone.

If you train a new puppy to sit, roll over, or give a high five, do you give the puppy a treat only when the puppy can do the trick after weeks' worth of training? No, you give the puppy the treat if he makes progress.

You have to treat yourself similarly. When you slowly start to step out of your comfort zone, you should reward yourself, even if it means watching an episode of your favorite Netflix series after spending 10 minutes in the company of your neighbor. As you expose yourself to these experiences more, the reward should become less, because you are normalizing it. Think of the moment when the puppy can roll over without being asked more than once. They don't even need a treat anymore; they just do it. Now the trainer can move on to a new trick.

When you have normalized your one experience, you will probably find it a lot easier to accomplish, and you won't need a treat for something that is easy. You have reached the outcome you want. Try something else that is new and uncomfortable, like joining a club in school.

The effort is important, but remember that you are working towards an outcome.

Taking Daily Action to Overcome Shyness

Make it a goal to speak to someone new every day. It doesn't have to be a grand conversation—start small. Ask a classmate about their day, compliment someone's shoes, or simply greet your neighbor. These are the kinds of small daily actions that can make a HUGE difference over the long term.

You can start in a grocery store (when you have to tag along with your parents) by greeting people. You can even just smile at kids you pass on your way to go sit down in the cafeteria for lunch. Start off simple.

You may stumble over your words or encounter someone who doesn't engage the way you hoped. That's okay. Not every one is going to be picture perfect (or even close), but it's about getting comfortable starting up conversations.

By taking these daily steps, you're not just practicing social skills; you're rewriting the narrative in your head that you can slay the shyness monster! You're not the shy kid who can't speak up; you're the brave soul who dares to strike up a conversation. With each new person you talk to, you're making the shyness monster weaker and weaker, until finally one day, you can slay it for good.

Smile More

If you are in a public place surrounded by masses of people all in close proximity, smile at people when you pass. Don't go and deliberately smile into their faces or wave at them like you are long lost friends; just give a subtle smile if your eyes catch theirs as you pass.

At the beginning, it might be just as awkward as giving them hugs. As a matter of fact, it probably feels like you never ever want to smile at someone ever again because no one is smiling back. It is not because you are smiling and greeting them that they aren't smiling back at you: They are suffering from first person syndrome. It is not your responsibility or your superpower to control people and how they react, but the least you can do is initiate.

What is the reward for smiling at random people? It's uncomfortable, you might think they think you're weird, and sometimes, you may feel a bit defeated because they don't smile back. However, there's also a good chance you might have just made their day a whole lot better! That in of itself is a great reward for you. When you help others or make others feel good, you also feel good.

Think of the way you feel when someone smiles at you in public: You feel affirmed and positive. They noticed you. You can give yourself a pat on the back for making someone's day. You did well.

The great thing about practicing social skills in a grocery store is the fact that not a single person will remember you tomorrow. In their heads, you don't even have a name, so by the time they get home, you will be a distant memory because they have other things and other people to worry about at home. You could pull faces in the grocery store at them for all they care–they will not remember you or anything you do. This should give you a little bit of relief, as a lot of fear and shyness comes from a fear of being remembered as a fool.

If you are done spending enough time out and about, smiling and interacting with strangers, treat yourself! Go grab a doughnut or a Starbucks hot chocolate, anything your heart desires! You just stepped out of your comfort zone. You just did something huge for your mental health as well as for your future! You are one step closer to being a rockstar, a lawyer, a doctor, or the person you want to be!

Generous Hearts Receive Good Vibes

Once you get comfortable with smiling, you can push things further by reaching out to help others. Of course, this will take a bit more energy than just smiling and waving, but it will be exceptionally more rewarding, because by helping, you are making a difference in someone's day.

You can start small, by offering to walk your grandad's or your elderly neighbor's dog. You can also reach out to local charity clubs and organizations in your school or in your neighborhood. They often arrange events where you can volunteer at homeless shelters and retirement homes, the places where people are forgotten completely. The difference between smiling at a stranger and helping is that the people you help will remember you forever as someone who made a difference in their lives.

This is your chance to prove that you are different and that you are not the klutz you think you are. By helping in a situation like this, even if it means ladling soup in a homeless shelter or playing bingo, you are stepping out of your comfort zone and making someone else's day a lot better.

Not only will you spend some one-on-one time where you can listen to other people's stories, a notorious comfort zone for an introvert, but you also get to learn what type of people they are and how much they actually do not care about you and your overthinking mind.

Spending time with people who are neglected and less fortunate than you can open your eyes to a whole new picture. There are bigger problems in the world than just being worried about something silly you did or said because you were distracted. There are people in the world that need clothes, attention, care, love, and compassion, and none of these qualities benefit from overthinking, overanalyzing, stress, worry, and fear.

You need to be fearless to help, because you are a part of a bigger picture with a bigger meaning. You aren't just the NPC in their lives; you are the healer, the difference maker.

When you help people, you also get something called "helper's high." This phenomenon happens when your body releases dopamine, or the feel-good hormone. If you help someone, you are not only trying to do something outside of your comfort zone by interacting with them, but you are also rewarding your body with feel-good hormones—because you deserve to feel good!

Being shy can hinder many parts of our lives and sometimes scare us to think that we are not reaching our full potential. If you are shy and scared to audition for that part in the school play, to be in the school band, or to greet the new kid to make friends, you are taking away purpose and the feeling of belonging from yourself.

We all want to fit in and belong somewhere. If you try to step out of your comfort zone to speak to people and volunteer, which means you have to talk to someone you have never met, engage in conversation with them, and share information about yourself, you are extending your feelers and finding your purpose.

Having a purpose is awesome. When you have a purpose or a goal, and are actively progressing towards it, it gives you true fulfillment. That feeling alone is a remarkable reward for something as small as helping out.

Do What Scares You

Eleanor Roosevelt once said, "Do one thing every day that scares you." If you do one small, scary thing at a time, it means that you are slowly but surely helping yourself become used to stepping out of your comfort zone. It is like slowly dipping your toe in the water that is icy cold. After dipping your toes into the water a few times, you won't even notice the drop in temperature, and your body will be comfortable.

Why do you want to step out of your comfort zone when your comfort zone is so warm and fuzzy (and sometimes comes with hot chocolate, a bed, and a TV show)? Sometimes, your comfort zone is not just your bed or your house—it is the way you think, your mindset, or an activity.

Stepping out of your box is like math…no, not boring! There are different kinds of math: geometry, calculus, statistics, and algebra. The only way you are going to get better at math is not by just doing one type of math, but practicing all of it and exposing yourself to a little bit of every type of math, which makes you a better mathematician.

Olympic athletes also have to step out of their comfort zones to grow in their careers; a great example is Michael Jordan, who started out as a basketball player when he was in college. After nine years as one of the best players in the NBA, Michael abruptly stopped playing in 1993, at the peak of his career, giving up basketball to play minor league baseball. The last time he played baseball was when he was in high school, thirteen years ago! The fact that he hadn't played in such a long time did not stop him from trying. Then he returned to the NBA.

A year later, Jordan returned to the Bulls to lead the pack. He averaged 30.4 points per game. He led the Bulls to remain undefeated with 72 wins for the season, taking down the Seattle Supersonics. He bagged another three titles before finally retiring.

If you don't step out of your comfort zone, you might miss your passion and purpose for the rest of your life. If Michael Jordan did not go off to try different ventures, he would not have realized his true love and passion: basketball.

Give Yourself Options

It is scary trying new things—like running downstairs in the middle of the night to get a glass of water scary…but it doesn't have to be.

If you want to step out of your comfort zone, try giving yourself options. Instead of bombarding yourself with major changes in character, try new things slowly. Say, for instance, that your goal is to make new friends. Give yourself two or three options on how to make them. Your options could look something like this:

1) Play Minecraft and greet someone playing with you. Ask them if they want to build a house with you.

Online games are a wonderful way to expose yourself to people without having to look them in the eye. You only hear a voice. You don't need to know their names, where they are from, or what they had for dinner. You might learn all these things as you work at kindling a friendship, but if the friendship doesn't work out, you will probably never see them again. It spares you the overthinking factor—you never have to think about them or the moment again, because you don't see them.

2) Join a club in school.

This option is probably the scariest one, but it is the most rewarding. When you go out and join a real-life club, you are exposing yourself to direct commentary, direct eye contact, and a lot of pressure. But once you break down these barriers and slowly introduce yourself to the group every week, the space becomes familiar and even comfortable. It's only hard at the beginning to break out of your box.

3) Compliment the girl with the cool dinosaur pencil case in geography class.

This one might be a complete shock to your system because it takes a lot of effort to say something first, but at least you are saying something nice. Handing out compliments will not only make you feel like a good person because you are making people's day, but also because you might have started an entire conversation about dinosaurs!

The important thing is to get out of your comfort zone whenever you get the opportunity. If you step out of it every day for the next 3 months, I promise you'll be unrecognizable by the end of it.

Conclusion: It's Your Time

Your gremlins are only scary when you see them in the dark, but when you put the light on, they look like cute, fluffy teddy bears on the great big diet you put them on.

It *really* sucks being shy. But do you know what sucks more? Not being able to do all the things you wanted to do because some ghost of your past is stopping you.

If you do not take full advantage of your future, you will spend days in and out of a retirement home one day, wishing you had done all these things when you were younger, when you were energetic, and when you had the time. When you reflect back on this time of struggling with your shyness, you will be proud of the fact that you could overcome it and come out even stronger on the other side.

It is time for you to take full advantage of your future. Take responsibility for your shyness, even though a lot of outside influences could have made you shy. It is not your fault that you're shy, but it also is.

Once you can take advantage of all the parts of you that make you shy and put them aside like an old toy on a shelf once you're done playing with it, you will be unstoppable. It is your time to audition for the play, to join the band, and to show everyone exactly who is boss on the sports field.

For all you know, there will be a kid out there one day looking up to you to answer the exact questions that you have now. Only then you will have the answers, but until that day comes, you have a lot of time to solve all the problems you need to solve.

Leave Your Feedback on Amazon

Please think about leaving some feedback via a review on Amazon. It may only take a moment, but it really does mean the world for small authors like myself :)

Even if you did not enjoy this title, please let me know the reason(s) in your review so that I may improve this title and serve you better.

From the Author

As a retired school teacher, my mission with this series is to create premium educational content for children that will help them be strong in the body, mind, and spirit via important life lessons and skills.

Without you, however, this would not be possible, so I sincerely thank you for your purchase and for supporting my life's mission.

Don't forget your free gifts!

(My way of saying thank you for your support)

Simply visit **haydenfoxmedia.com** to receive the following:

- 10 Powerful Dinner Conversations To Create Amazing Kids

- 10 Magical Affirmations To Help Kids Become Unstoppable in Life

(you can also scan this QR code)

More titles you're sure to love!